Natalie Ann Hughes is a 22-year-old from Liverpool. She has loved writing since a young age. Natalie has struggled a lot with various mental health issues. She hopes to tell her story through poetry on how mental health can affect people and also hopes people can relate to it, too. Natalie has spent years in mental health facilities, such as hospitals, and in the present moment, is recovering, and still learning as a person, as we all learn new things every day. The past few years have been a battle for Natalie, but she hopes her work can make people understand how mental health can take a toll on people's lives. She believes we still have so much to learn about mental health.

Natalie Ann Hughes

Mental Health Matters – Volume 2

We all start small but
eventually stand tall

AUSTIN MACAULEY PUBLISHERS™

LONDON • CAMBRIDGE • NEW YORK • SHARJAH

Copyright © Natalie Ann Hughes 2022

The right of Natalie Ann Hughes to be identified as author of this work has been asserted by the author in accordance with section 77 and 78 of the Copyright, Designs and Patents Act 1988.

All rights reserved. No part of this publication may be reproduced, stored in a retrieval system, or transmitted in any form or by any means, electronic, mechanical, photocopying, recording, or otherwise, without the prior permission of the publishers.

Any person who commits any unauthorised act in relation to this publication may be liable to criminal prosecution and civil claims for damages.

A CIP catalogue record for this title is available from the British Library.

ISBN 9781398428669 (Paperback)
ISBN 9781398428676 (ePub e-book)

www.austinmacauley.com

First Published 2022
Austin Macauley Publishers Ltd®
1 Canada Square
Canary Wharf
London
E14 5AA

I would not have got through this journey without the help of support workers in different settings such as hospitals, supported living, and the help of my amazing family, my mum, dad and partner, who are my rock, and all my family who have been there for me every step of the way: my sister, nan and grandad. They have all helped me gain confidence and grow as a person. I will be forever grateful to my nan who is sadly not with us anymore, who I know is my guardian angel watching down on me every step of the way. I would not be the person I am today without my family – they are everything to me. My beloved grandad who recently passed away and is in my heart, and here in every weather.

Once again depression you've been told,
However you really do have a hold.
It stings so bad then pain,
I'm just trying to keep sane.
It's hard to deal with everything you throw at me, my wounds are open,
Unfortunately, here's no magic potion.
No potion to make me feel better than yesterday,
Why are you here, you must leave, don't stay.
The shame, the blame,
That my life is a game.
I'm stuck in a cell,
I ring and ring the bell.
Nobody comes to the door
Because they give up on you like before.
Because you're saying the same old stuff
Please go, I've had enough,
I might seem tough but I'm fragile and a little weak
And it's not help that I want to seek.
The reason being I've had help before but I'm ashamed of the way I feel,
Take me to church to pray this pain will heal.

I've lived here,
A life through fear.
An illness stealing millions of lives every day,
At home you must stay.
Stay at home,
Contact your family on the phone.
Stay 2 meters apart they say,
We pray for a better day every day.
When will it all be over, god what's going on?
Look at that woman just lost her baby son.
Look at the pain as we can't visit our loved ones out of our household,
This virus is big and bold, stealing lives off many, some young some old.
Will it make us look at our world in a different way, a time we will never forget?
Will it make us have a different mind-set,
That nothing lasts forever, things can be temporary.
There's pain now but hope we see,
Will it make us reunite as a world and teach us to never take things for granted again?
Do this together and keep the mind-set we can.
We can do it together,
Coronavirus is like a stormy weather.

It may come back, it might leave,
It's caused an uproar, caused millions to grieve.
A lot to go before their time,
Oh let's pray one day we will be okay again, be fine.
A time we have cried, missed our family members,
Feel like we have had many cold Decembers.
We will rise again for sure,
Don't worry, you'll knock on a loved one's door.
To everyone on the frontline; you're so brave,
Thank you for our lives you save.
Being young and being free,
What a dark future I couldn't see.
Because I used to be so happy before this,
My old life I will miss.
Lollipops and a candy cane,
Who'd have known life in the future was full of rain.
What would your 8-year-old self say to yourself now?
Would she recognise the girl who feels so low?
Trips in the park,
Now all I see is the dark.
Who'd have known depression could steal my teenage years right away,
Just about getting through the day.
A life of dread,
Listening to what my demons said.
Remember all your dreams, now they're shattered,
A mind so lost, a mind so scattered.
Your dreams have disappeared,
This life is everything you've ever feared.
God, what have I done to deserve such a hard time?
Why do I feel far from fine.

Depression destroys,
I wish I was 8 again playing with toys.
When life was actually bright,
Now absolutely nothing is right.
I miss you childhood where once I saw the good.
Growing up really is a trap,
In my mind my demons tap.
They're pulling me in by a rope,
Sorry Mum and Dad, I can't cope.
I'm not your little girl anymore.
I'm a monster now with a claw,
I'm a monster who's been took over, possessed.
And at the same time I'm just looking for a rest,
Naps in the day to shut the dread out my mind for a while.
There's a lot of weight on my shoulders, a whole pile,
The thing that's painted on is a smile.
A mask and my life a task,
A task where I have to drag my way up the obstacles from every direction.
Depression is like a nasty infection.
Spreading throughout my body but not like a broken leg with a cast,
No, that's where I wear the mask.

Dad, you're everything a dad could be,
How precious you are, I hope you see.
You're everything a daughter could ask for,
Each day I love you more and more.
When you're happy it makes me complete,
I'll tell you a story about my dad, take a seat.
My dad is everything, a hero, he makes me complete.
Dad, being on your shoulders as a child was the highest place in the universe,
You're amazing, you taught me to be myself, to be diverse.
You've always had faith in me since the day you held me in your arms for the first time ever,
You are the sun in rainy weather.
You always cheer me up when the world is a scary place,
I remember when I was a child and we would play games, me you would chase.
My love for you is never ending,
You've been on every journey with me even when life was bending.
Picked me up when I fell,
You mean the world to me, from this poem I hope you can tell.
The love a daughter has for her father will never end,
From everything to an inspiration to a best friend.

Words can't describe how much I love my dad,
In this life he blocks out the bad.
When I look I see someone who is the light,
I listen to your advice and you're always right.
A father will be a best friend from the start,
And is the first person to have such a big effect on your heart.
So, Dad, you are precious, family is everything,
When I'm broke, you fix the link.
The link that wants me to stop going,
You're the support like in a boat rowing.
Rowing and guiding me to the right way,
Dad, you really make my whole day.

Mum, this poem is to show just how much I love you,
The hardest times in life you've helped me pull through.
You will have a key to my heart always,
You're the light in rainy days.
I appreciate you so much, nothing beats a mother's touch,
For you I'd walk a thousand miles.
When I think of our memories, I'm full of smiles,
The bond between us is unbreakable, so surreal.
When I look at you, a warm heart and love is what I feel.
My best friend, I'll be with you every step until the end.
People like you are hard to come by,
I love you unconditionally that is no lie.
I'd walk the highest mountain for you, Mum,
You're beautiful, stunning and a bundle of fun.
I'd walk anywhere for you from as big as an ocean to as small as a pond,
No one will ever break our unbelievable bond.
You make me believe in myself,
Always there to help.
I'm so lucky to have you by my side,
You inspire me when I want to hide.
You guide me to the right way,
And when you smile, it makes my day.
You make me feel safe in the darkest night,

In my life you are the light.
So, Mum, I hope you know how much you mean
Because me and you are a team.

Guess what, my life means something and I'm going to get on track,
To my demons I'm going to never look back.
I'll fight with everything I have inside,
I'll get past the scary part off the rise.
Yes I'll ride it out,
Show you, mental illness, what I'm all about.
Why do you always have your say,
Guess what, I'm going to make you pay.
Because I'm young and have a whole life ahead,
One day I won't dread getting out of bed.
I'm not saying it will be easy at all,
But I'll pick myself up every time I fall.
I know I have a long way to go through this storm,
But my aim is to be on top form.
Every time you come fighting and knock asking me to play,
I'll say no, not today.
Asking me to play your deadly mind games, I'll say no,
I'll catch you like a ball and you I will throw.
Throw you far away so I can build a wall,
I will stand tall.
The wall will stop you from ever coming back, a wall where you won't be in sight,
Yes, I'll bite.

I'm not here to play around,
No you won't win, it's not a dead body that will be found.
Look how many lives you've destroyed, you're not adding me on to the list,
I'll fight with my fist.
You may choke me and it will be hard to come up for air,
But this is not fair.
No it's not fair on me or others whose life you took,
I'll finish this book.
And I'd be happy if I just helped one person who was going through some kind of struggle in life,
Watch out for mental health whether it's your mum, son, daughter, nan or wife.
Depression has a nerve,
But I'm rebuilding myself, it's a new kind of birth.
A birth where I rise,
Where I'll no longer wear a disguise.
Because I know one day you won't win,
I'll throw old dark times out in the bin.
I'm not where I want to be yet,
But one thing, I'll get strong is my mind-set.
And I know one day I'll feel like me again,
I fight for it every single minute, every second.

Sometimes I just don't feel like me,
I'm broken but you would never see.
Constant feelings of dread,
Please, depression, leave my head.
My mind feels torn and broke all the time,
This is one struggle of a climb.
What does happy feel like,
What does it feel like to be normal, to be fine.
I fight, trust me, I really do,
But this is one big struggle to get through.
Wrapped up,
But I'll smile look.
Yes, that's all it takes to hide a nightmare,
Really life is so unfair.
What did I do for life to kick me down to rock-bottom,
Feeling like I'm worth nothin'.
I try to stay strong,
But, believe me, this suffocation has been here so long.
I'm losing control,
I've lost my soul.
Waking up and dreading the day ahead,
Lying sobbing in my bed.
Maybe I need time to heal,
But I'd do anything to not feel.

I'm haunted by depression,
One more therapy session.
I'm lying on the floor dying,
Will somebody just believe me, I really am trying.
I'm dying piece by piece,
I wish my mind overthinking would give me some peace.

Depression, why are you always there,
Anxiety, why do you stop and stare.
You stare at me and take all the good things far away,
Looks like you're not here for a visit, you're here to stay,
Because every time I wave goodbye,
You come back and spoil my day.
My whole world changed when you came along,
Like the stereo player is on a repeat on a sad song.
I want this mood to die,
Believe me that is no lie.
Because If I live I'm in torture every day,
In my mind you lay.
Please, I'm begging you to leave,
Because my old happy life I grieve.
You're like a constant rainy cloud raining right through,
You're a constant nightmare too.
My mind is sad, my mind is deep,
What do I have left to keep.
A broken heart falling apart,
It's like my heart's stopped and won't start.

Walk through the rain,
The thing that's real is the pain.
I look up to the misty sky and I pray,
I pray tomorrow will be a better day.
The pain latches onto me and I can't breathe, I'm gone by far,
Smoking this cigarette full of tar.
The only thing it takes to hide a broken person is a huge smile,
Why in life do I always fail,
The ship's gone, it already set sail.
I tried to jump on to a sunnier destination somewhere else but fell, can you tell?

Look, this story is from when I fell.
Wait a second, I'm back,
For depression I found a hack.
I'm a warrior who has been through a battle that was so difficult so hard,
Pacing my back yard.
But the truth's coming out that I'm back with a boxing glove,
Depression, I'll kill you with love,
Because I'm not ready to be above.
I've learnt a few lessons, a few tasks,
Depression get reading the facts.
Is that all you got?

You think this is all I have? I think not.
I've let you take over time and time again I'll scream and give everything I got inside,
In you I will not confide.
No I know you won't win,
I have thick skin.
Come on I'm waiting,
Suicide I'm not debating,
As I'm strong I'm humble my life is precious
So, depression, read this message.

Lately these voices in my head are drowning,
Feeling like I'm frowning.
Where am I meant to go,
Death is that way I guess so.
What door, show me the way,
Because why should I stay?
Sometimes I just want to run away.
A lesson learnt this life isn't for me, my pain isn't visible,
But in a world full of people, I feel invisible.
Is this all there is,
I pump up, I fizz.
I'm getting angry because I don't see the point,
My body's aching joint by joint.
Seeing things on the wall,
Writing a suicide letter, even making a call,
My demons stand so tall.
They torment me, making all the good things disappear,
Making me think I'm a burden and why am I here.
The fact I'm worthless they are making it clear,
Making me live a life of fear.
But I'll just carry on like I always do,
But help me god this is one big blue,
Give me a sign to be happy, a clue.

But all the happiness is being sucked far away where I can't reach,
I should practice what I preach.
I write about being positive when I'm stuck,
One minute, let me rip up this whole book.
Why do I write,
Why infect, am I even in sight.
Because I'm a monster, that's what I am,
And the problem is I'm becoming my demons' number one fan.
Because I'm doing as they tell me like they're the boss,
Why do I give a toss.
Give a toss about this miserable life,
Someone tell me where is a knife.
Because I'm done, I'm gone, I throw down this pen, I'm good at hiding pain,
But honestly now there's too much rain.
My stomach is in knots, I feel sick,
Like someone has hit me on the head with a brick.
Believe me, the weight is killing,
Self-harm is thrilling,
Someone is in my mind drilling.
Drilling all the happiness away and bringing the sad to the surface,
Sorry but what is my purpose?

Who'd have knew this day would come,
The day I'd be behind the trigger of the gun.
The day the tables had turned right around the other way,
Yes, today is my day,
The day I'd make mental health pay.
I just pulled the trigger and shot depression to pieces,
I ironed out the creases.
The creases what lived in my head, the demons that lived within,
You're on a line and it's thin.
Because I'm learning how to defeat you, depression,
Getting behind the trigger was a blessin'.
The times we've had where you've ripped me apart,
Since the very start.

Guess who's in charge now, well it's me,
I'm at sea.
And I can see the destination,
I'm docking at the station.
The station of recovery,
Where I made a discovery.
A discovery along the way that I'm stronger than you by far,
It's been up and down like elastic on a guitar.
There's been hard times where I couldn't see nothing at all,
But now I'm at the edge off the cliff and I won't fall.
I'll jump right up high,
Right to the sky.
Depression you're weak and I'm strong,
I fought piece by piece all along.
Always remember a storm doesn't last forever,
Remember after a rainy day the sun always takes over the bad weather.
Shines so bright,
My sun will shine, so depression you're not even in sight.
I'm writing this from deep within,
I feel like a monster, an abomination in my own skin.
I'm feeling far from fine,
I don't fit in this town.
Constant regret,

Depression, I'm actually not over you yet.
Everything good I have, every happy emotion you suck away,
Anxiety and depression, how long is your stay?
Because looks like you're back for a fight,
Why do I write.
Shouldn't I just give in,
I'm far away from home.
Will you leave if I raise my tone?
No, you just knock me clean out,
I'll try to fight back, I'll shout.
I thought happy ever after would exist,
I clench my fist.
Here I am feeling like this,
Angry emotions for letting you sneak your way in.
I'll just let you win.
Because do I have energy to fight back, no,
I'll give it a good go though.
Wait, why did I think I could go up against you,
When you've won this battle through and through.
I surrender, I don't have the energy,
Maybe need a remedy.
You're like one thousand weights on me,
I'm broke enough, can't you see?
You continue to crush,
This feeling I can't brush.
I'm dying for a normal life, even just one touch.

Depression, don't pretend to be in front,
You have not won so get the point.
I don't intend to waste everything God has given,
Because guess what, I have an interest in livin'

You've tried to win time and time again,
But I'm beating you with every line I write with this pen.
I'll say it again, I have an interest in living my life,
One day I intend to be a mum and wife.
You don't get the final say, I do,
Although you've tried through and through.
Tried to strip everything away,
But guess what, I'm having my say.
Oh I swear I'll be strong,
You've controlled my life far too long.
You don't have my best interest,
You're a coward, a pest.
Trying to take all the good away,
Depression, this is not your day.
It will never be your way ever,
You're cunning and clever.
However I just dodged your bullet, you can't catch me, I'm one step ahead,
I will welcome the day as I awake in my bed.
I will smile and live,
Because this life of mine has a lot of good to give.
Get my flow? I'm not feeling low,
No I'm on top of the world because I defeated you depression,
Looks like I just taught you a lesson.
Now stay far, far away, don't come back, no, there's no loop hole,
I've retrieved the life you stole.
A feeling that won't go,
A constant low.
One which I can't shake,
My mind continues to bake.

I'm falling,
My heart pouring.
I envy others wishing I was like them,
One problem adds on to the stem.
The stem of a flower,
Dread every hour.
I'm breaking down,
Wearing a constant frown.
Tears coming from everywhere,
In the street people stop and stare.
Because my scars show,
Dying from head to toe.
Worrying about the littlest thing,
The sadness will sting.
If I had one wish, it would be to not be depressed,
Or for my mind to have a rest.
Constant overthinking every night,
Hiding my tears as I switch off the light.
I want to flip the switch and feel no more,
My guts are hanging, my heart is raw.
Raw from pain that lasts forever,
This is more than being just sad just being under the weather.
How long will these lows last I ask,
My mind will overlap and multitask.
Oh just a poet trying to write,
But this is one constant bad night.
On the surface I'm happy, I'm calm,
Inside there's a voice saying cut that arm,
In my head there's an alarm.

Changing destinations, crippled thoughts late at night,
The same old path in sight.
Each night I walked down the same path,
Each night I'd barely smile, barely laugh.
I'd walk each night into the same trap,
One where my thoughts would overlap.
The same old story I'd climb out the same space,
One where depression became my base.
Where anxiety became my best friend,
One where I wanted my life to end.
One night I changed my destination,
One where I destroyed a creation.
One where I said goodbye to my destination,
Where I waved goodbye to that abomination.
The abomination was the dark hole that sucked me in with.
great pleasure, I waved goodbye,
Now I would live life like I was high.
Not high on anything else except feeling alive,
No longer in this hole would I dive.

This is it now, throw everything I've got, hit some speed,
Depression and anxiety are full of greed.
They tried to take everything I have,
I'll play it cool and just laugh.
I've got plans that are bigger and better,
Rip up that suicide letter.
I'm changing tides moving on,
Maybe one day I'll have a daughter or a son.
Because you won't beat me, I'm on my way to the top,
You think you can come back, well I think not.
It's emotion what I write,
Success is in my sight.
I write my rhymes ever so deep but that's the best give everything,
Because I know I won't sink.
You've defeated too many people and I'm doing this for them,
Give everything I can with this pen.
It will be hard, that I won't deny,
But my ladder's up to the sky.
Can you see me climbing, no one can knock me down,
Hello smiles hello happiness kick down that frown.
I put everything on the paper,
Well, depression and anxiety, I'll see you later.

This moment is precious surreal,
Strong is what I feel.

The feeling is gripping on,
The weight of the world on my shoulders weighs a ton,
A world so cruel,
Where your mind can be a harsh tool,
A tool that's the root of all evil known
Where your own voice raised an angry tone.
The weight is unbearable I am weak,
Help I won't seek,
Because I'm scared,
I remember a time I cared,
But that's a very long time ago,
Now I'm past low,
I'm hiding my darkest fears inside,
In whom do I confide, or do I continue to hide,
Holding my head high when I'm dying,
Believe me, I'm done with lying,
Lying that I'm fine,
When this pain is ripping me apart like a shredder far from fine,
The pieces are flying, that's right I'm dying.

Goodbyes are hard when people have made such an amazing impact on you,
When they've been there and the mud and dirt they helped you come through,
I'll miss everybody here like mad,
But it's time for a new chapter in my pad,
Time for new beginnings and time to move on, the people around me have been amazing,
But I've got new stars to follow and they're gazing,
So shiny so bright,
Thank you for being there through my fight,
In the hardest times ever, you helped me see what life has to give
Made me realise I want to live
This world is full of amazing people like you all,
Bounced me back when I would fall.
Guess this is not goodbye, it's see you later, I'll never forget,
In my heart you'll always have a place, that's set.
Set up for you all so special and warm,
You helped me through a gigantic storm.
Each off you inspire me,
Now I'm like a bird I'm free.
Free to fly and you guided me which way to go, let's see what the next chapter offers like a book.

And from me to you the very best of luck,
I can't thank the staff at Brunswick ward enough for everything the times we have.
I'll hold like a photograph all the memories we shared one day, we will look back at these times and laugh.
I'll never forget the times we had,
Especially the good but even the bad.

I've got to get this down on paper,
No motivation, I'll do it later.
Silent tears, a sadness that I can't shake,
Paint a smile that's fake.
Why is life so harsh, I'm falling apart every break I take.
But you'd never know,
Depression captures me, is this all there is for me, I guess so.
Because every time I think I'm there,
Life knocks me down, it's so unfair.
Why should I feel this way when there's people much worse off than me,
I'm breaking down but you'd never know, never see.
A sadness that makes everything seem so pointless, a feeling of dread,
If only you could see inside my head.
It's a constant war zone, one in which I feel so alone,
But I'll act okay, make a clone.
A clone which isn't really how I feel,
One in which the bad sides I conceal.
The truth is I'm used to feeling this way,
Used to wanting an end to come to the day.
I'm so sad that it hurts, stings so bad,
When I close my eyes, I see the life I wish I had.

But I can't let my family down so I'll carry on and pretend everything is fine,
If I'm being honest, it's breaking my heart writing this line.
Is happiness too much to ask?
I can't go on with such an empty heart, something is missing,
Like a time bomb I'm fizzing.
Why does everything feel so hard?
Honestly I'm tired,
Two shots fired.
Fired at me, from this darkness I try to flee,
I'm emotionally done, no words can describe how down I actually feel,
But I'll laugh, it's no big deal.
But deep down it is my heart that's broken.
I feel every dark emotion, hide it away,
If I had one wish, I'd wish I didn't dread the day.
Dread each hour,
I'm like a dying flower.
Where I try to bloom,
But I can't unfeel this gloom.
Please god, why is my life like this all the time,
I pray to just be like everyone else fine.
This poem is close to home, really is from down deep,
These stairs I'm climbing are way too steep.
I'm worthless, that's what I am.

I can't do this even though others think I can.
Depression has now got a hold,
Feeling so numb so cold.
Trouble coming to pay a visit,
Depression is back, really is it?
I thought that might be you,
Know you would come back and take everything too.
It feels like a million knives scraping against my bone,
One more sad song on my phone.
Why can't you leave me alone?
And unfortunately relapse looks like your back knocking me down,
Highlighting my frown.
Why can't I make my family proud,
My demons scream over and over, they get loud.
I knew you'd be out there lurking somewhere,
Because you just don't care.
Care about destroying everything good,
Just because you felt like it and knew you could
In a world full of people how could I feel this alone.
Halls of darkness sleepless nights,
Constant battles scary fights.
Please just go,
My anxiety is racing from to to

These voices in my head,
A constant feeling off dread.
Looks like I'm back to the beginning,
I'm like a hamster on a wheel replaying and spinning.

One day I hope to sell out my own book,
For others to look.
That recovery is possible because I'm breathing proof.
The times that I've had, the people I've met,
All at different stages of recovery unique with their mind-set.
The rich, the poor who couldn't find the right door,
But came out the deep end to the shaw who shut out the past and times before.
Yesterday's gone,
Time to change tides, time to move on.
Changing tides is difficult, it won't be easy, it takes will-power,
But you will bloom like a flower.
Keep looking up,
If you're struggling with life, I wish you good luck.
I've been in your shoes before,
My heart I would pour but feel so alone.
With tears in my eyes I'd write a poem,
I could express myself like never before,
Take people on a tour.
Depression, you're a cheat,
Anxiety, you're a thief.
But you have not won,
Because I've found the sun.

One minute I hope you get the flow,
I gotta start living in now.
I hope my poems give you goose pimples make you feel,
Hope my books are a big deal.
These are words from the bottom of the heart if you're struggling speak out,
Get it all out if even you want to shout.
Somebody out there now reading this who's low, I've been in your shoes plenty of times,
That's the whole reason I write these rhymes.
My ambition once fell apart, no motivation,
Poetry is the greatest creation.
No I'm writing this from the other side,
I'm up in the clouds, I send my love down then through the clouds I glide.
I was with them every single minute,
I lay next to Dad in my bed.

Is this a life we're living cos I'm so confused,
I'm on my mat fused.
A life where children and others are living in poverty,
In one where I'm happy the things that wears off is the novelty.
How can a world be so evil, the poor suffering
It's outrageous,
How can people be expected to be courageous,
This feeling is contiguous.
The feeling of sadness,
A world with badness.

I'm broken, broken,
Broken by every word that has been spoken.
Scared to live, scared to die,
Watch the day out the window pass by.
I want this day to come to an end,
Maybe darkness has become my friend.
These wounds hurt so bad,
To say goodbye to the day I'll be glad,
I'm anxious, lost and sad,
Why does is hurt so much, so raw,
My brain is sore.
I see others and I wish I was them,
One tear turns to ten.
Then here come the puddles,
My demons give me cuddles.
Wrap me up, I scream let me go, they choke me around my neck,
Just snap out of it, I won't be a sec.
That's what people want me to do, snap out of it,
But my mental state isn't fit.
No it's far gone,
My demons I run from.
My heart's racing, my head's pacing like a merry-go-round spinning,

Yes, depression, you're winning.
What did I do to deserve to live this way,
Please depression, leave, don't stay.
I wish I could forget,
But this one troubled mind-set.
Does your mind ever drive you crazy,
You're exhausted and people think you're lazy.
A normal life you're chasing,
But look in the mirror, the demons are facing.
They hide in your eyes,
Cuts on my thighs.
Cuts on my arm,
Here goes the alarm.
Yes another sleepless night,
Don't turn out the lights or it will give me a fright.
I blow out the candles silently with a smile upon my face,
On my new shoes I tie the lace.
Today a day I've been waiting for a long time, a happy day, with family about,
The best day ever without a single doubt.
I smile as they all cheer,
My dad drinks a beer.
Time to celebrate,
My uncle shows up late.
I put my arm on Mum's arm,
Everybody seems so peaceful, so calm, the music plays,
My sister's smile sets off sunshine rays,
Everybody together at their home.
Here goes the phone,
My grandmother saying she couldn't face it because something is missing from the day.

Everybody goes home, on my bed my dad will lay.
Like he has done every day for the past year,
With great fear.
I put my arm around my mum and hold her hand,
But it slides through like sand.
I'm with them all in some kind of special way but they can't see,
But now I'm free.
I wipe a tear from Dad's face,
A day which we celebrated together but the world not being my base.
No I'm writing this from the other side,
I'm up in the clouds, I send my love down then through the clouds I glide.
I was with them every single minute, I lie next to Dad in my bed,
I rub my little sister on the head.
I smile as I place a kiss upon my Mum's cheek waving to her goodbye,
With them through every happy memory through every sigh.
I'm gone but I'm always here with you all,
I'm in heaven now, a place where I won't fall,
And, Mum, I seen for the first time my baby sister crawl.
Through every heartbreak they have, I'll be near through every tear,
I'm right here.